US MILITARY

ARMY RANGERS

BY CHARLES MARLIN

Apex is distributed by North Star Editions:
sales@northstareditions.com | 888-417-0195

Produced for Apex by Red Line Editorial.

Photographs ©: Shutterstock Images, cover, 6, 27; Sgt. Paul Won/US Army/DVIDS, 1, 16–17, 20; Sgt. Eric Kestner/US Army Reserve/DVIDS, 4–5; Spc. Garrett Shreffler/US Army/DVIDS, 7; Photographer's Mate 1st Class Greg Messier/US Navy, 8–9; Hugh Charles McBarron, Jr./US Army Center of Military History, 10–11; US Army Spc. Justin Young/DVIDS, 12–13, 28–29; Bettmann Archive/Getty Images, 13; Sgt. Jaerett Engeseth/US Army/DVIDS, 14–15; Capt. Veronica Aguila/DVIDS, 18–19; Spc. Steven Hitchcock/US Army/DVIDS, 21; Spc. Wyatt Moore/US Army/DVIDS, 22–23; Spc. Nikayla Shodeen/US Army/DVIDS, 24; Pfc. Eric Overfelt/US Army/DVIDS, 25; Wayne V. Hall/Pennsylvania National Guard/DVIDS, 26

Library of Congress Control Number: 2025939209

ISBN
979-8-89250-803-2 (hardcover)
979-8-89250-832-2 (paperback)
979-8-89250-887-2 (ebook pdf)
979-8-89250-861-2 (hosted ebook)

Printed in the United States of America
Mankato, MN
012026

NOTE TO PARENTS AND EDUCATORS

Apex books are designed to build literacy skills in striving readers. Exciting, high-interest content attracts and holds readers' attention. The text is carefully leveled to allow students to achieve success quickly. Additional features, such as bolded glossary words for difficult terms, help build comprehension.

TABLE OF CONTENTS

CHAPTER 1

NIGHTTIME ATTACK

An airplane flies across the night sky. Inside the plane, a green light flashes on. Army Rangers begin to move. One by one, they leap out of the plane.

Soldiers who jump from planes or helicopters are called paratroopers.

The Rangers **parachute** down to the ground. Then they gather in groups and prepare to attack. They run toward an enemy airstrip.

An airstrip is a long, flat stretch of land where planes can land and take off.

Army Rangers may fire rocket launchers at tanks or thick walls.

MANY WEAPONS

Rangers often carry **assault rifles** and pistols during **missions**. Some shoot sniper rifles. These guns can hit enemies from far away. Rangers may use rocket launchers as well.

The enemy soldiers are surprised. They run away. The Rangers take over the airstrip. US planes land on it. They bring more troops and supplies.

FAST FACT

Rangers often work with other military groups on difficult missions.

Army Rangers and US Marines took over an airstrip in Afghanistan in 2001. The US military later used it as a base.

CHAPTER 2

RANGERS THROUGH THE YEARS

The Rangers are a **special ops** group. They're part of the US Army. They formed during the American Revolutionary War (1775–1783).

General Daniel Morgan led a team of Rangers during the American Revolutionary War.

Military raids are quick, sudden attacks on enemies.

The Rangers disbanded in the mid-1800s. But they restarted to fight in World War II (1939–1945). Rangers gathered information on enemies. They also carried out raids.

WORLD WAR II

During World War II, Rangers took part in D-Day. This attack brought US troops into France. Rangers also fought in Asia. They freed US soldiers who had been taken prisoner.

During D-Day, thousands of soldiers landed boats on the coast of France. They included about 1,000 Army Rangers.

From 2001 to 2021, Rangers carried out many missions in Afghanistan.

The Rangers went on pause a few more times after that. But they helped US troops fight in Asia and the Middle East. Some fought **terrorists**. Others freed **hostages**.

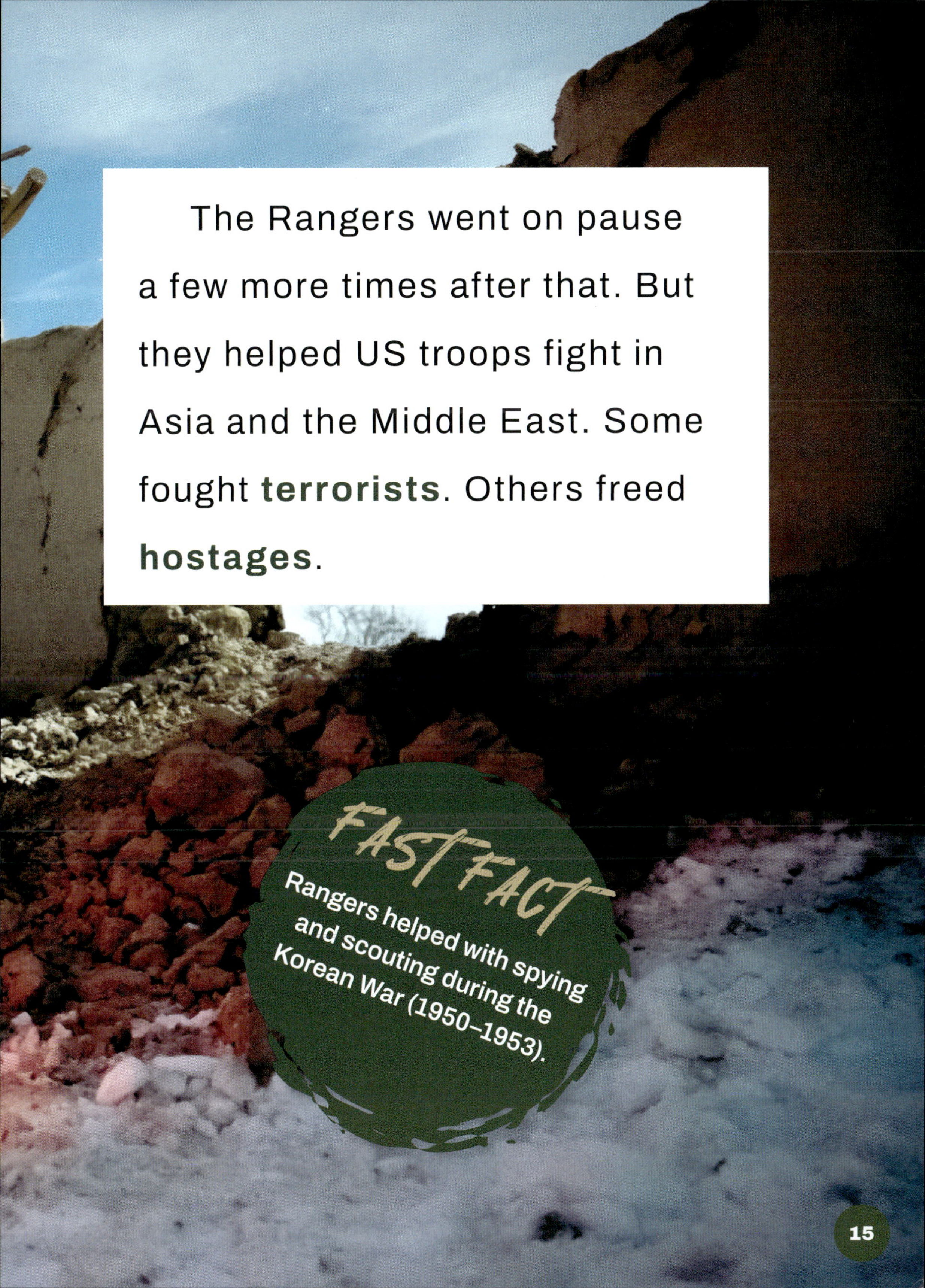

FAST FACT

Rangers helped with spying and scouting during the Korean War (1950–1953).

CHAPTER 3

TESTS AND TRAINING

To become Rangers, US Army soldiers must pass an eight-week course. It has two phases. Phase 1 involves a series of tests. They put soldiers through **stressful** situations.

Only 33 percent of soldiers pass the course to become Army Rangers.

Soldiers train by carrying heavy packs for many miles.

During Phase 1, soldiers also do difficult workouts. They run, swim, climb, and fight. Soldiers practice working in teams, too.

FAST FACT

Many of the Ranger tests take place outdoors.

Rangers practice entering buildings and fighting in tight spaces.

In Phase 2, soldiers build new skills. They practice shooting weapons and using **explosives**. Soldiers also learn ways to find and capture enemies. They do practice missions to show their skills.

FINAL TEST

Phase 2 ends with a test. Some soldiers pretend to be enemies. Other soldiers must take them down. Army leaders watch. They decide which soldiers pass.

Rangers keep training after they pass the course. They keep learning new skills.

CHAPTER 4

MANY MISSIONS

Army Rangers do several kinds of missions. Many involve attacks. Rangers may destroy enemy weapons or take over buildings. They may also spy or do rescues.

Rangers sometimes slide down ropes to reach the ground quickly.

Today, there are about 3,500 Army Rangers.

Rangers do missions around the world. Often, they must respond quickly. So, soldiers are split into different battalions. These groups are sent to fight. Other teams support Rangers during missions.

FAST FACT

One support team cares for hurt soldiers. Another focuses on creating attack plans.

Ranger medics learn how to help soldiers who get hurt.

The RQ-28A is a small drone. Soldiers can use it to spy on enemies.

The fifth battalion is the newest. It formed in 2017. Its members focus on intelligence. They spy on enemies. And they attack enemy computers.

NEW TOOLS

Rangers often test and use new technology. They have some of the most-advanced tools and vehicles in the US Army. For example, they have powerful **grenade** launchers.

The Stryker is an armored vehicle. Its thick sides help keep Rangers safe during dangerous missions.

COMPREHENSION QUESTIONS

Write your answers on a separate piece of paper.

1. Write a few sentences explaining the main ideas of Chapter 4.

2. Which part of Ranger training sounds the hardest? Why?

3. During which war did D-Day take place?

- **A.** American Revolutionary War
- **B.** World War II
- **C.** Korean War

4. How many battalions do the Army Rangers have?

- **A.** one
- **B.** two
- **C.** five

5. What does **disbanded** mean in this book?

The Rangers ***disbanded*** *in the mid-1800s. But they restarted to fight in World War II (1939–1945).*

- **A.** broke apart
- **B.** got back together
- **C.** completed a mission

6. What does **intelligence** mean in this book?

Its members focus on ***intelligence****. They spy on enemies.*

- **A.** training hard
- **B.** ignoring missions
- **C.** getting information

Answer key on page 32.

GLOSSARY

assault rifles

Guns that can shoot many rounds of ammo very quickly.

explosives

Devices that can blow up, such as bombs.

grenade

A small bomb that is thrown or launched.

hostages

People held as prisoners until certain demands are met.

missions

Tasks or plans with specific goals.

parachute

To jump from high up while wearing fabric to slow one's fall.

special ops

Military groups or missions requiring extra skills and training.

stressful

Tense, overwhelming, or pressure-filled.

terrorists

People who attack and scare others to reach their goals.

TO LEARN MORE

BOOKS

Banks, Anita. *US Army*. Apex Editions, 2023.
Hamilton, John. *United States Army*. Abdo Publishing, 2021.
Marlin, Charles. *Tanks*. Apex Editions, 2025.

ONLINE RESOURCES

Visit **www.apexeditions.com** to find links and resources related to this title.

ABOUT THE AUTHOR

Charles Marlin is an author, editor, and avid cyclist. He lives in rural Iowa.

INDEX

ANSWER KEY:
1. Answers will vary; 2. Answers will vary; 3. B; 4. C; 5. A; 6. C